RAIL TRANSIT PHILADELPHIA
TWENTY COLORFUL YEARS
1969-1989

HENRY ELSNER AND RICHARD VIBLE

N.J. International Inc.
1989

Before the SEPTA era: Red Arrow Car No. 84 on an Ardmore Express Run, West Chester Pike at 69th Street Terminal. (EL)

Front Cover—Forty years separate three generations of SEPTA streetcars on display at the new Elmwood carhouse, July 28, 1984: Kawasaki Industries 9000 (1981), St. Louis Car Co. 2109 (1948), and St. Louis Car 2054 (1941). (EL)

Rear Cover—For a brief period traditional Red Arrow equipment shared duties with the first Kawasaki cars. At 69th Street Terminal on August 20, 1982, brand-new 112 is about to leave, while Brill-built 7 (1941) and 84 (1932) wait on the ready tracks. (HE)

ISBN 0-934088-24-1

Published by N.J. International, Inc. 77 West Nicholai St. Hicksville, N.Y. 11801

No. 7608

Printed in Hong Kong

PREFACE

The city was green, the suburbs were red—the reference is not to political predilections, but to traditional transit car liveries in the greater Philadelphia area. For years the city streets were ruled by the green cars of the Philadelphia Rapid Transit Company (PRT) and its successor Philadelphia Transportation Company (PTC), while the Philadelphia Suburban Transit Company (PST) used the color indicated in its less formal title, Red Arrow Lines. The monotony was relieved only by a minority of orange rear-entrance cars in PRT days, and later by an occasional public service advertising car, a few pieces of work equipment, and the drabness of the old rapid transit cars.

All this was to change with unification, beginning in 1968, under the Southeastern Pennsylvania Transportation Authority (SEPTA). Partly by design, more often by fortuitous circumstance—sometimes disastrous—a rainbow of colors would appear on city and suburban vehicles in the following twenty years. As this is written, a standard livery finally seems to have stabilized, although some variety is still provided by the trim on the stainless-steel cars of the rapid transit lines and the PATCO (Port Authority Transportation Company) interstate fleet.

Seeking a new image after its formation, SEPTA experimented with a number of liveries, polling the public with regard to three of them. Standard schemes were adopted, then discarded, one rather quickly, the other after several years. So many cars were lost in a 1975 car-barn fire that substitute equipment hastily purchased from Toronto was put in service still in that city's colors. Bicentennial celebration of the Declaration of Independence brought a distinct livery to a select group of cars, as well as a special visitor from England and an abortive restoration project. Rehabilitation of the remaining PCC fleet brought yet another color scheme to Philadelphia streets. New cars built by Kawasaki, delivered in 1981-82, came with the new livery—later modified in proportions if not in color. Finally, emergency conditions on the former Philadelphia & Western (P&W), now officially designated the Norristown High Speed Line (NHSL) again

brought second-hand cars, in 1986, this time from Chicago. They entered service in three color variants.

The same changes in livery were not always found on both city and suburban divisions; the various paint schemes overlapped in time and most were not applied to all cars, so that an amazing variety could at times be seen simultaneously.

It is easy to become accustomed to events, even somewhat unusual ones, when living through them; the eye of an outsider is often needed to bring them into focus. The editors owe thanks to Jack La Russa for insisting that a record of colorful, changing, Philadelphia traction is worthy of more than a local audience. The resulting presentation, it should be stressed, is intended neither as a history nor as a comprehensive equipment roster, and it makes no claim to evaluate policy. It is an attempt to record, within limited space, the truly remarkable kaleidoscope of colors appearing on the Philadelphia transit scene over the past two decades.

Special thanks are due to Edward Springer, not only for his unusual photographs, but for his critical comments and useful suggestions. And Charles P. Long reviewed the captions, resolving a number of ambiguities.

Henry Elsner, Jr.
Richard Vible
Philadelphia, Pa.
30 September 1989

Photo credits: (EL) ELECTRIC LINES collection, including work by the late Raymond Muller; (RV) Richard Vible; (ES) Edward Springer; (HE) Henry Elsner; (RJ) Russell E. Jackson; (LR) Lawrence Ryan; (RG) Russell Greco; (JB) Jack Bailey; (EWS) Edward W. Sharretts.

CITY TRANSIT DIVISION

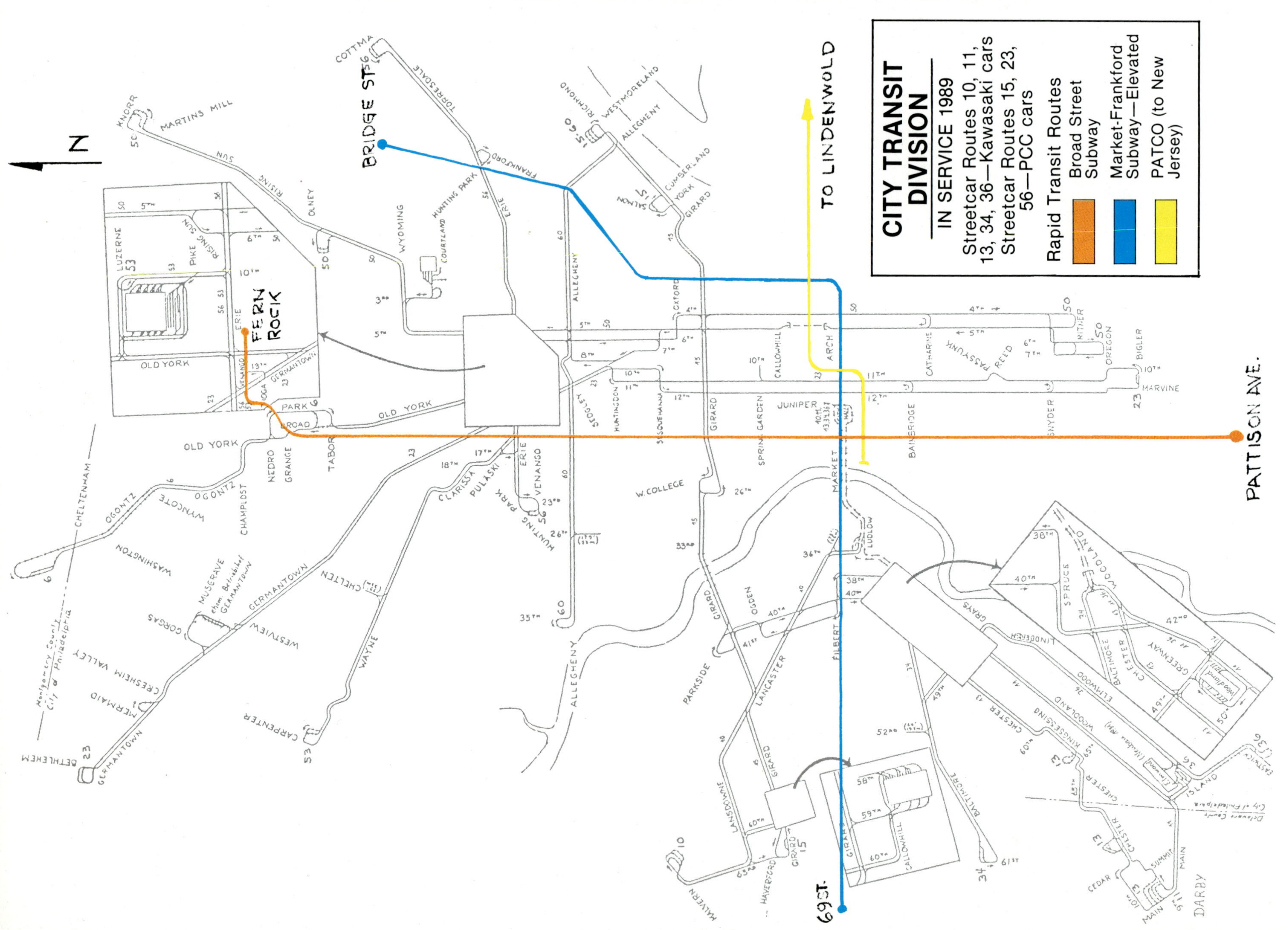

The color scheme and special roll sign on 2054 echo those used when PCC cars were introduced to Philadelphia in 1938. The car, a slightly different model than the original series, was restored in 1978 to celebrate that 40th anniversary. With Independence Hall in the background, Fifth Street at Chestnut, summer, 1978. (RV)

A favorite for special trips, 2054 is southbound on Route 6, Park and Chew Avenues, November 10, 1985. (EL)

On the transfer table at Woodland shops, July 28, 1984. (EL)

Wayne Avenue was the first Philadelphia route to receive PCC cars; 2074, built in 1941, is from the oldest series to survive into the SEPTA era. Wayne and Carpenter, January 1976. (RV)

Car 2640, still with a Golden Glow headlight, Wayne Avenue at Arbutus, October 1969. A SEPTA emblem has been applied, but the car carries the standard PTC colors—green and cream with maroon beltrail. (RV)

At Germantown Avenue and Old York Road, September 6, 1976. The two cars on the left are operating on Route 23; the car on the right is a pull-out from Luzerne barn. (ES)

Cars continued to be repainted in a simplified version of the traditional livery well into the SEPTA period. Obviously fresh from the paint shop, 2658 at Woodland carhouse, December 4, 1979. (EL)

All-electric 2743 sports a new dash and SEPTA emblems, but otherwise shows signs of age and hard service. Germantown Avenue and Old York Road, May 18, 1982. (EL)

Car 2118 westbound on Allegheny at Second, August 22, 1968. Both Route 60 rail service and the brick factory buildings are now only memories. (ES)

PTC purchased 40 PCC cars from Kansas City Public Service in 1954-55. The all-electric cars had a unique body design, lacking the familiar standee windows. Car 2283 southbound on Rising Sun Avenue near Adams, September 1968. (RV)

One of the few paint variations to appear during the PTC reign was the Zoo car, 2667. Route 15, Richmond loop. July 1965. This special decoration lasted only one season. (ES)

Another PTC special—the Safety Car, 2128. At Summit and 9th streets, Darby, on the final day of operation of shuttle route 62 as a separate entity. January 23, 1971. (RV)

Shortly after inauguration of SEPTA operation, several buses and streetcars were repainted in three experimental color schemes. Blue car 2733 bore the shortest-lived of the trial liveries. At 12th and Vine on July 4, 1969. (ES)

Popularly called "the banana car," 2168 carried its distinctive color for a longer period; 54th and Lindbergh, March 20, 1973. (EL)

Several cars received the tan livery; 2718 at 63rd and Columbia, August 1970. (RV)

Car 2111 westbound on Girard at 42nd in September 1969. (RV)

Air-electric 2565, Seventh and Susquehanna, June 1969. (RV)

During this period, a gold color scheme also appeared. At the 40th Street subway-surface portal, August 11, 1969. The first of University of Pennsylvania's highrise towers is under construction. (ES)

Three of the four city division cars given the gold livery were also extensively rebuilt and modified. Turn-signal dash lights and bus-type roof markers are visible on 2176, at Fourth and Pine, March 1970. (RV)

Car 2176 on its inaugural run in January 1970. At the Route 53 loop, Wayne and Carpenter. (RV)

The interior of 2176 featured a carpeted floor and blue vinyl seats in a novel arrangement. The seat covering material and colors were to become standard; the seating pattern and the rug were not. January, 1970. (RV)

Like 2176, 2165 received center-exit push-doors. The car's interior had plastic seats. On July 7, 1973, 2165 is southbound on 40th Street at Locust on the subway-surface diversion route. (EL)

The wide shroud at the trolley base was to accommodate experimental air conditioning, later removed. Eastbound during reconstruction of the 15th Street underground station. (EL)

The gold livery proved difficult to maintain. The next stage saw tan car 2565 selected for a major overhaul and given another trial paint scheme, promptly dubbed "Gulf Oil" by cynics. Others felt the design and colors well-suited to the lines of the air-electric car. The first orange car eastbound on Girard at Corinthian, May 1973. (RV)

Car 2054—later given the silver commemorative livery—at Ogontz and Champlost, August 1977. (RV)

The orange color scheme was the first of the new ones to be applied over several years and to a substantial number of cars. All-electric 2749 at Courtland shops, February 23, 1974. (EL)

On the Route 15 cutback loop, under I-95 at Richmond and Cumberland. July 7, 1973. (EL)

Color treatment of the doors was changed in a later version of the orange livery. Car 2758 southbound on Germantown Avenue at Berkeley, October 4, 1984. (EL)

As one of SEPTA's contributions to the 1976 Bicentennial Celebration of the Declaration of Independence, 27 of the former Kansas City cars were repainted in a new red, white, and blue livery. Two cars were named after each of the 13 colonies, with three for Pennsylvania. "South Carolina," car 2267, southbound on Germantown Avenue at Gravers Lane, April 9, 1982. (HE)

Interior of the first Bicentennial car, 2251. Emblem on the ceiling at back reads "Philadelphia Historical Trolley." Red and blue seating was not repeated for the series. Luzerne carhouse, June 1976. (RV)

"Delaware," 2252, Ogontz and Walnut Lane, July 1978. (RV)

Cars 2259 and 2728 pass on Snyder Avenue and Fifth, June 1976. Route 50, to which the Bicentennial cars were originally assigned, passed through Independence Park with its colonial-era historic buildings— far from this location in South Philadelphia. (RV)

A few of the Bicentennial cars later received a simplified partial repaint, eliminating the state name, the stars, and the Bicentennial emblem. When no longer needed by SEPTA, 10 of the cars were sold to a Maryland broker. Car 2279 is about to leave Luzerne carhouse in October, 1986. (EL)

On loan from Blackpool, England for the Bicentennial was an open "boat" trolley. It ran on a special "Historic Loop" using route 50 tracks; Fourth Street at Pine, summer 1977. (ES)

In October, 1975 a fire destroyed two-thirds of the Woodland carhouse, ironically sparing equipment in dead storage but taking active cars, leaving SEPTA with a major equipment shortage. (ES)

In response to the Woodland fire, 30 cars were bought from Toronto, and pressed into service still in that city's colors. The units were all ones which Toronto had itself bought second-hand. Former Toronto, former Kansas City 2245 westbound on Allegheny Avenue near Kensington, June 1976. (RV)

Another ex-Kansas City, ex-Toronto car, 2240, passes standard air car 2525 in front of the former Richmond carhouse, Allegheny Avenue at Salmon, in April 1976. (RV)

Several of the Toronto/Kansas City cars were repainted in standard colors. They could be distinguished from the cars purchased directly from Kansas City by the distinctive TTC "advance lights" on the roof and the folding doors with which Toronto had replaced the original blinker type. Car 2240 again, Broad Street at Grange, September 4, 1977. (RV)

Nineteen of the cars bought from Toronto were Pullman-Standard vehicles which had run in Birmingham, Alabama. Two of these cars pass at "K and A" (the intersection of Kensington and Allegheny Avenues), Market-Frankford elevated station, September 4, 1977. (RV)

A chance lineup of equipment at Luzerne carhouse in July, 1976 shows the variety of transit liveries then to be found in Philadelphia. (RV)

SEPTA's specially-equipped (and painted!) "Training Trolley" on Ogontz Avenue near 66th, June 1980. (RV)

Clever use of window and door openings outlined the superimposed single-truck car image. Rising Sun and Knorr, June 1980. (RV)

An appropriately-decorated car marked the occasion of a "Farewell to Air Cars" special trip in the summer of 1982; at Luzerne carhouse. The trip was a bit premature, but this type of car soon disappeared, as did many all-electrics, reflecting service cuts and route abandonments. (RV)

Battered and graffiti-laden, 2105 represented SEPTA rail service at its nadir. "Nowhere to go but up"? At Haverford and 61st, March 1977. (RV)

In 1980, a program was begun to completely rebuild 112 PCC cars for service on the remaining surface-only routes. Car 2758, in Woodland shops, reveals the extensive nature of the work. (HE)

Work has yet to begin on 2732, while 2799 and 2740—presenting a glimpse of another new paint scheme—are near the end of the rehabilitation process. (HE)

Car 2791, not part of the overhaul program, received an "unofficial" version of the new livery, with a different dash treatment. (ES)

Car 2715 was the prototype rehab; at Park Avenue and Olney, July 1982. The car was retired in 1989, as its planned 8-year service extension had expired. (RV)

An excursion in May 1981 could include refurbished 2122 along with Toronto/Birmingham 2309, air-electric 2571 still in green, and Bicentennial 2255. At Ogontz and Medary, southbound. (RV)

At the northern terminal of Route 6, Cheltenham and Ogontz, May 10, 1983. (EL)

As the seal and ribbon indicate, 2728 was the 100th car rebuilt (and the only one to have its PCC headlight wings reinstalled). Luzerne carhouse, October 1986. (EL)

A new era began for Philadelphia's five subway-surface routes with the arrival of 112 Kawasaki units from 1981 to 1982. Point of delivery was at the end of Route 36. September, 1981. The block number displayed on the windshield indicates the car number to be applied later, here (90)03. (ES)

Cars 9001-9002 on a run to test clearances for multiple-unit operation. Rising Sun and Butler, June 29, 1981. (ES)

An excursion with 9052 on March 13, 1982 took the car to locations not served by this type of equipment. On Fourth at Callowhill. A PATCO car in the background is beginning its run over the Benjamin Franklin Bridge. (EL)

Still off-location, 9052 shows the difference in body dimensions between new and old as air car 2662 is passed on Germantown Avenue at Glenwood. (RV)

The large area of blue proved difficult to touch up after minor abrasions, so once again the standard livery was changed. Car 9067 in the new livery, with 9084, at Route 10's Malvern loop. February 7, 1987. All Kawasaki cars now have the narrower trim. (HE)

City work cars, like passenger units, were green in the pre-SEPTA era. Motor flat W-40 in Center City on Route 23, May 1966. (ES)

A change to orange improved safety for vehicles usually on the streets at night. Line car D-39, built by SEPTA from subway work motor T-17. On Sixth crossing Allegheny, August 3, 1986. The center freight door on the other side of the car was kept. (ES)

At the Woodland Avenue subway-surface portal, car W-62 ex Toronto. U of P's high-rise dorms now dominate the scene. (ES)

Car W-56 appeared in the Luzerne lineup photographed in 1976. By May, 1984 it had lost its front skirting and has a bare lightbulb for a headlight. Woodland subway-surface portal. (HE)

The last two PCCs in the overhaul program became line cars. Woodland shops, September 25, 1987. (RJ)

BROAD STREET SUBWAY

The two traditional types of Broad Street subway cars were the North Broad units of 1928, like number 78, and the South Broad cars of 1938, like freshly painted 166. Fern Rock shops, October 21, 1983. (EL)

South Broad car 161 is at the rear end of a train which has just emerged from the subway at Fern Rock. July 23, 1975. (EL)

North Broad 126, Fern Rock, September 1, 1972. (EL)

Restored to original appearance, North Broad car number 1 headed a special train on November 13, 1983. (EL)

At the other end of the train was South Broad car 166. November 13, 1983. (EL)

Twenty-six Brill cars bought in 1936 for the line to Camden over the Benjamin Franklin Bridge were favorites of many because of their distinctive mid-1930s styling and deep-cushioned bucket seats. Car 1020 at Fern Rock, October 28, 1967, slightly more than a year before the SEPTA and PATCO eras would begin. (EL)

After purchase by the City, the bridge cars were integrated with Broad Street subway operations, and received the new livery adopted for that line. Car 1024 heads a train leaving Fern Rock for the subway, September 1, 1972. (EL)

A Bridge car in Bicentennial colors. Fern Rock, July 23, 1975. (EL)

Car 1014 in a more utilitarian livery. Fern Rock, March 12, 1982. (EL)

"Broad Street IV" is the official name for the Kawasaki type which replaced all older equipment. Trim color reflects the "Orange Line" designation. Fern Rock shops, July 1982. (RV)

Motor T-17, later rebuilt to surface line-car D-39. Fern Rock, July 1977. (ES)

CW-1 and CW-2, Fern Rock, August 1977. CW-1 has been rebuilt into a single-cab crane car. (ES)

MARKET FRANKFORD SUBWAY-ELEVATED

The stainless-steel fleet of Market-Frankford rapid transit cars was delivered in 1960. Front Street at Poplar, summer 1974. The elevated structure at this point has been replaced by median running in I-95. (RV)

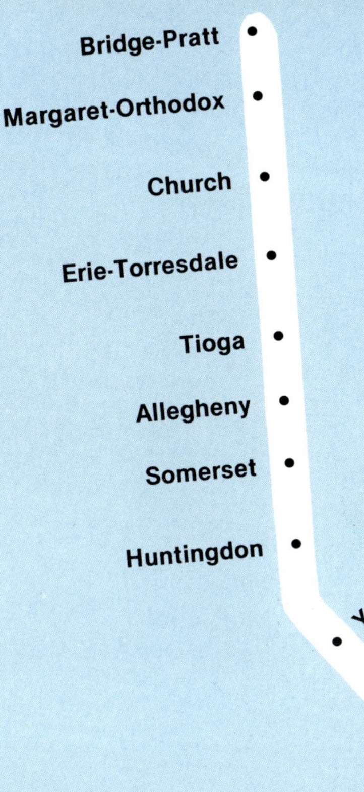

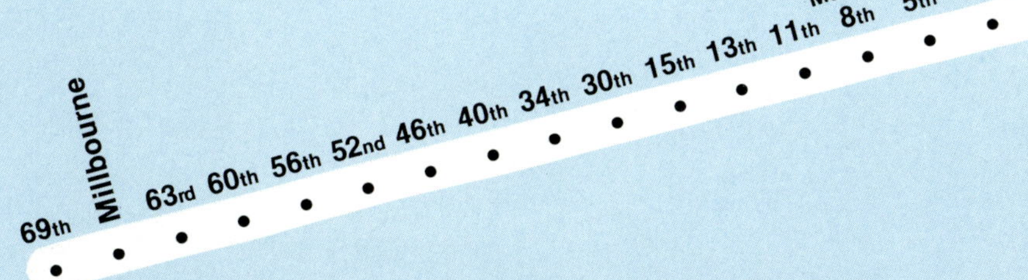

Under a 1980s overhaul program, completed cars received a thin blue stripe and "Blue Line" identification. Official color designations for the rapid transit lines, reflecting the tenure of former general manager David Gunn, were never popularly recognized. At 15th Street, eastbound, August 4, 1989. (RG)

Most of the color in the Market-Frankford line is on its work equipment. At 69th Street yard, August 2, 1975. Revenue car R-1 is a former Frankford passenger unit. (ES)

T-6 at work near Allegheny Avenue, May 1970. (ES)

W-37 with a rebuilt cab. At 61st Street, May, 1985. (ES)

RED ARROW TROLLEY LINES

In the postwar years, Philadelphia Suburban's trolley operation was dominated by the 14 St. Louis built cars delivered in 1949. The traditional red livery had several variations. Car 17's narrow windshield gave easier access to the wiper mechanism. Cars 17 and 24 are on West Chester Pike storage tracks which were once running rails for the West Chester and Ardmore lines. September 28, 1972. (EL)

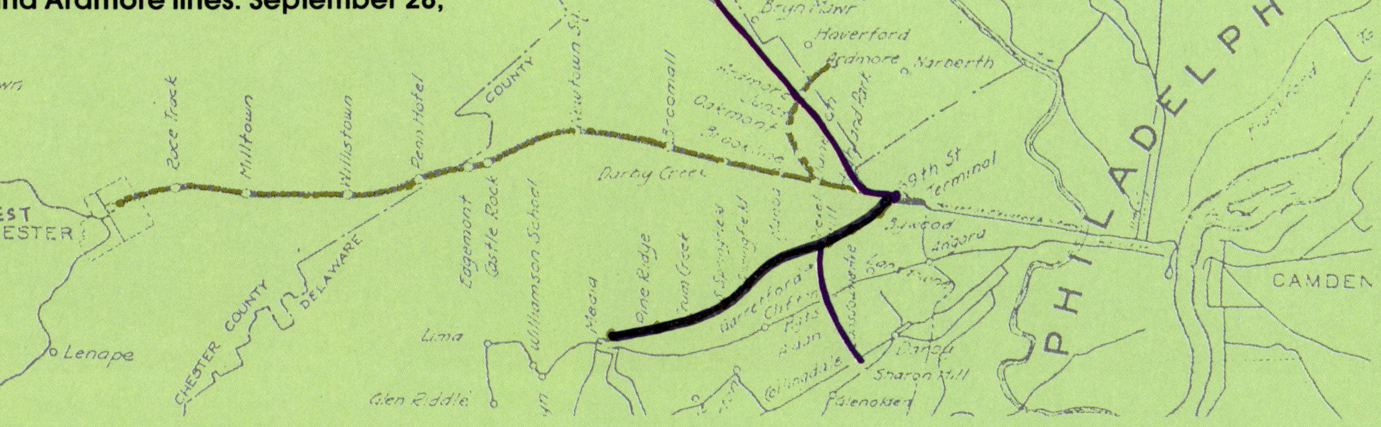

A two-car train of St. Louis units, 15 and 16, near Drexelbrook, is headed toward 69th Street on August 11, 1970. Large SEPTA stickers cover the old Red Arrow logo. (ES)

Car 20 on the Ardmore line, June 1966. This route was abandoned on December 29 of that year, before the SEPTA reign began. (RV)

Red Arrow base service was shared with the last cars built by Brill, series 1-10 of 1941. Number 9 on State Street, Media, October 22, 1967. (ES)

Car 3 at South Ardmore on the Ardmore route, June 1966. (RV)

Only a handful of the big center-door suburban cars survived into the SEPTA period; the curved upper sash had been covered earlier by PST. Car 73 heads a two-car train at North Avenue, Aldan, on the Sharon Hill line in September 1970. (RV)

Some of each Red Arrow car type except the center doors received the gold livery. A two-car train at Congress Avenue, January 1973. (RV)

In the 69th Street yard, February 21, 1974. (EL)

The orange paint scheme was also adopted on the Red Arrow trolleys. St. Louis 23 on State Street, Media, August 1982. (RV)

Brill car 8 inbound on Garrett Road, February 8, 1979. (EL)

Ten high speed lightweights built for the West Chester line in 1931-32 were used chiefly for rush-hour service on the remaining routes after West Chester abandonment in 1954. Departing Drexel Hill Junction, headed for Media, April 1982. (HE)

Car 84 at the Congress Avenue stop, outbound from 69th Street, October 26, 1980. (EL)

Car 79 on the Smedley park bridge, March 14, 1982. (EL)

On the Ardmore line, inbound near Merwood, June 18, 1966 in PST red and cream. (ES)

THE MANY HUES OF CAR 80

Car 80 was the only one of the series to have all the small windows next to the platforms blocked off; 69th Street yard, September 28, 1972. (EL)

Shortly after it was repainted in orange, car 80 had a motor burn out and was withdrawn. A rare in-service view, on Garrett Road between Beverly Hills and Naylor's Run, February 1978. (EWS)

Recognize the blue car in a Hyundai television commercial? It's Red Arrow 80 in temporary paint, applied over a stripable rubber base. Delaware Avenue at Dock Street, September 1986. (RV)

Repainted in authentic livery, car 80 serves tourists at the Penn's Landing trolley line on Delaware Avenue along the Philadelphia waterfront. November 11, 1984. (EL)

Double-ended versions of the Kawasaki cars replaced all other passenger equipment on Media-Sharon Hill in 1982. State Street, Media, in August 1982. (RV)

Car 101 inbound at Smedley Park, April 1985. (JB)

The overhead line crew at work, State Street, Media, May 1974. (RV)

Red Arrow work equipment was a bright yellow under PST. Sweeper 4, on the Media line December 29, 1966, is now at the Arden, Pa. trolley museum. (ES)

NORRISTOWN HIGH SPEED LINE

For many, the Philadelphia & Western image was a Brill "Bullet" car on the bridge over the Schuylkill river. Between Norristown and Bridgeport, August 5, 1976. (EL)

- **Norristown**
- **Bridgeport**
- **King Manor**
- **Hughes Park**
- **Gulph Mills**
- **Conshohocken Rd.**
- **County Line**
- **Radnor**
- **Villanova**
- **Stadium**
- **Garrett Hill**
- **Rosemont**
- **Bryn Mawr**
- **Haverford**
- **Ardmore Ave.**
- **Ardmore Junction**
- **Wynnewood Road**
- **Beechwood-Brookline**
- **Penfield**
- **West Overbrook**
- **Parkview**
- **69th St. Terminal**

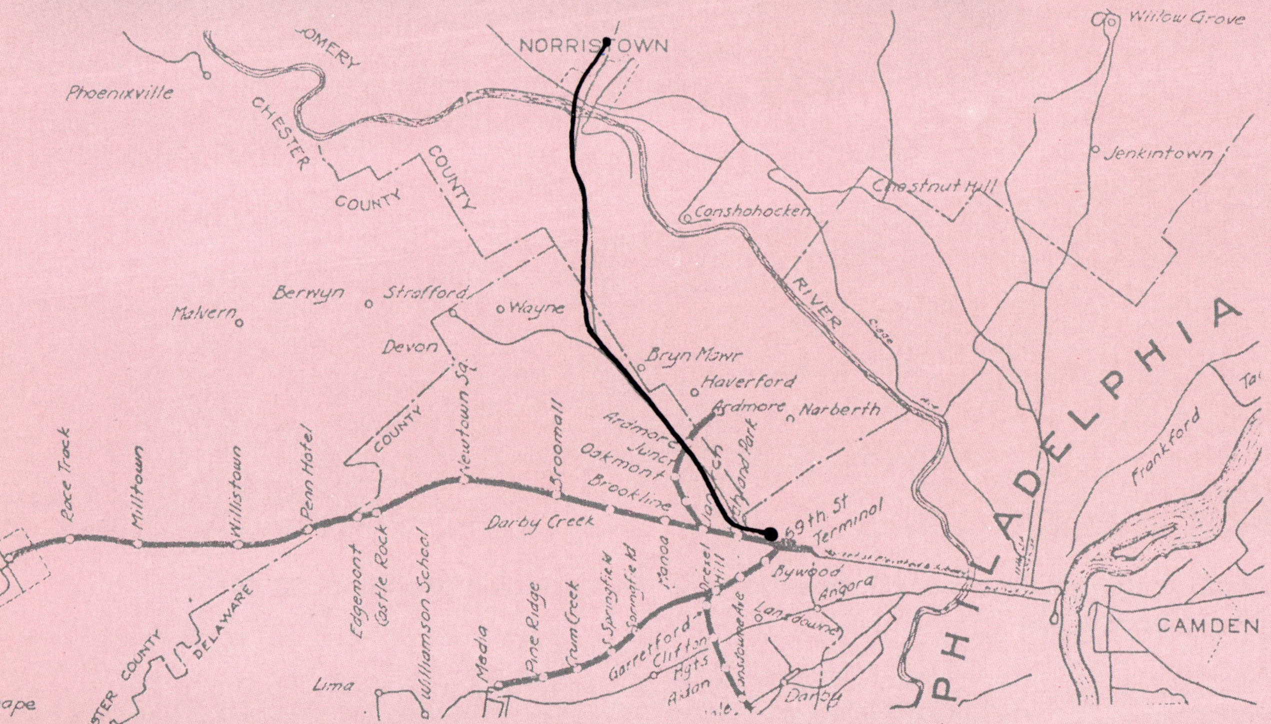

The 160-series "Strafford" cars, known by the name of the route they once served, shared work with the Bullets. Car 162 approaches the elevated Norristown station just out of sight at the right, on November 15, 1981. In 1989 this car was the last of its type—still in traditional red—in revenue service. The portion of the elevated structure shown was demolished in June, 1989. (EL)

Car 164 outbound between Conshohocken Road and Gulph Mills, May 1983. In 1986-89 the car was relegated to shop-switcher status. (RV)

The first, and only, tan livery on the P&W was given to 165. The color was judged so inappropriate that the car was repainted within weeks. Bryn Mawr, March 1970. (HE)

The next experimental livery, unique to the P&W, was an orange and white scheme given to several Bullet cars; 208 inbound at Beechwood-Brookline, December 15, 1974. (EL)

At about the same time, Strafford car 161 appeared in solid orange. At the Norristown terminal, Main and Swede streets, January 10, 1975. With the opening of a new station in June 1989, this portion of the elevated was dismantled. (EL)

Wynnewood Road, with 161 on a local turnback run, and Bullet 209 on an express trip to 69th Street. December 15, 1974. (EL)

A posed scene: Bullet 203 and a special "Reading Blue" train on SEPTA's ex Reading Norristown Regional Rail route, June 8, 1986. The new Norristown Transportation Center, serving the rail lines and local bus operations, was built just to the left of this view. (EL)

The publicity-conscious president of Philadelphia Suburban, Merritt H. Taylor, Jr., purchased the two Electroliner interurban sets from the defunct Chicago, North Shore & Milwaukee in 1963 for rush-hour service, complete with cocktail bar, on the P&W. The streamliners brought a distinctive color scheme to the route. One of the units, re-named "Libertyliners," outbound at Ardmore Junction in April, 1964. (RV collection)

SEPTA's only alteration to the Libertyliners was a change in emblems. Leaving Bryn Mawr, February 1972. The 'liners were expensive to operate and maintain, and were eventually transferred to operating museums in Pennsylvania and Illinois. (RV collection)

The current SEPTA standard livery was also adopted on the P & W: 208 and 209 at Wynnewood Road, November 15, 1981. (EL)

Accidents, age, and deferred maintenance finally overtook the line, leading to several months' shutdown of the P&W in 1986. Service was restored with the aid of two-car sets of PCC rapid transit cars bought from the Chicago Transit Authority. CTA 6139, in the Chicago Bicentennial colors, passes the P&W shop on December 19, 1986. (HE)

The oldest and newest P&W cars share the current livery: shop switcher 164 stands by as 6090, first of the CTA cars to be redone in SEPTA colors, is unloaded after delivery from the Woodland shops. At 72nd Street P&W shop, December 19, 1986. (HE)

Former Chicago 6079, in standard CTA green, on the rear of an outbound train at Gulph Mills, January 23, 1987. (RJ)

Plow 10 at Ardmore Avenue, February 6, 1978. In 1988 plow 10 was moved to the trolley museum at Orbisonia, Pa. (LR)

Steel 402 was purchased from Detroit with insurance money in 1943 after fire destroyed wooden 402, which was similar to 401 (next page). At Villanova substation in July 1969. Visible at left is the right-of-way of the former Strafford line. (ES collection)

Box motor 401 dates from the opening of the Philadelphia & Western in 1907. At 72nd Street shop, February 21, 1974. (EL)

Both work motors glisten in new paint at 72nd Street, April 6, 1988. (ES)

RESTORATION & PRESERVATION

Restored Peter Witt car 8534 (Brill, 1926) was intended for a Bicentennial "Historic Trolley" service which failed to materialize. The car was later made available for special tours and civic events; it is no longer on SEPTA property. At the Germantown Avenue and Bethlehem Pike loop of Route 23, December 9, 1978. (EL)

At 49th Street and Gray's Ferry Avenue, November 1979. (RV)

Red Arrow 62 was restored by President Taylor in the system's last year of private ownership and then donated to Maine's Seashore Trolley Museum. Drexel Hill Junction, January 17, 1970. At the end of that month PST operations became part of SEPTA. (EL)

Later, center door car 73 was in turn restored by SEPTA. On Garrett Road at Beverly Hills, December 15, 1974. The car is now used for work service. (EL)

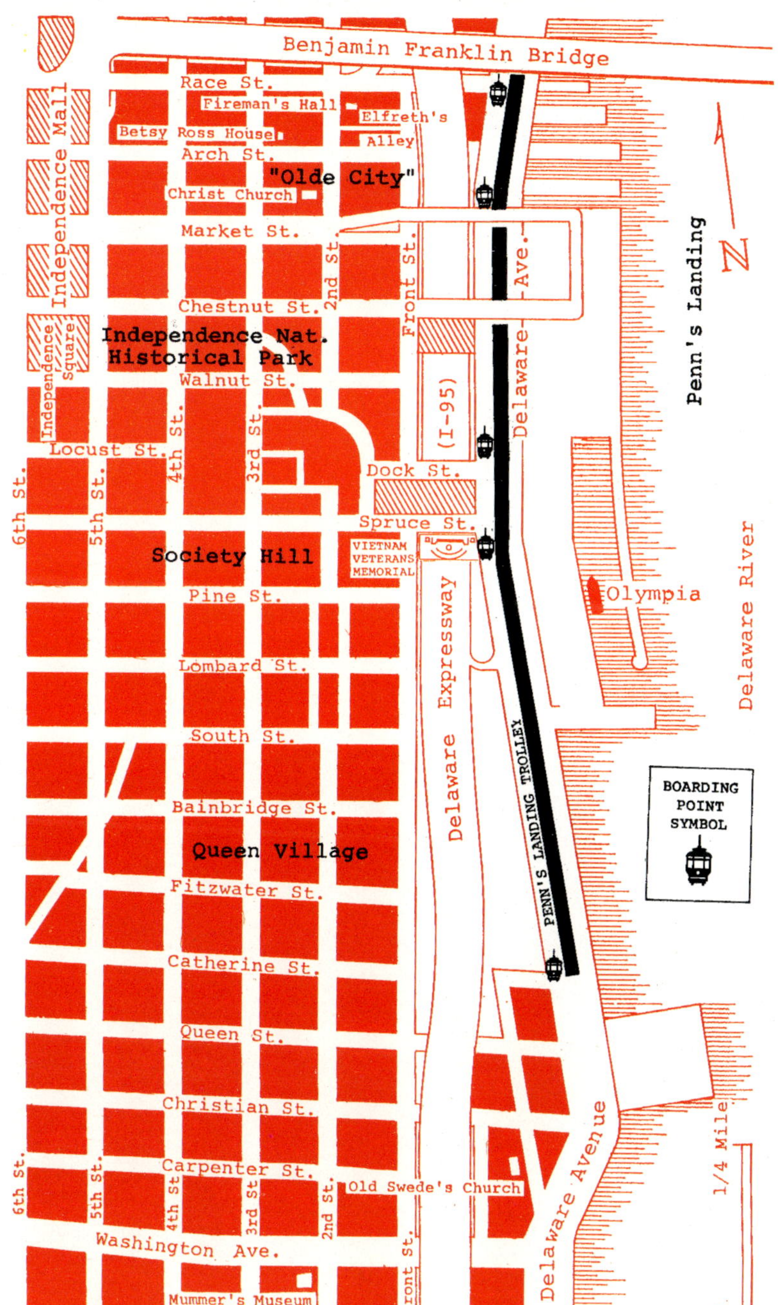

Several vintage cars operate at Penn's Landing on weekends from spring through fall. Car 26 (Brill 1918) is a "Hog Island" type built in World War I for PRT's shipyard service. It was sold to Red Arrow to relieve equipment shortage there during the Second World War, and has been restored in that company's livery. On Delaware Avenue, February 13, 1983. In the background is the Ben Franklin Bridge which carries PATCO trains to New Jersey. (EL)

Car 46, now on the Penn's Landing trolley line, is one of the cars which inaugurated P&W service. After many years as a work car, with baggage doors cut into the sides, it has been restored to original appearance. Delaware Avenue at Dock Street, November 11, 1984. (EL)

Henry Elsner, a transplanted midwesterner who has lived in Philadelphia since 1961, writes on electric railway topics.

Richard Vible, a native of Philadelphia with a longstanding interest in the history of the city and its transportation systems, is employed in the transit industry.

Outbound on Route 6, Champlost at 16th, August 1, 1972. (EL)